LOVER'S LANE

A COLLECTION OF ROMANTIC POETRY

MARK BENTLEY

For all those who found true love

Contents

Contents

Foreword

It is my pleasure to introduce you to the romantic poetry of Mark Bentley. His work is a testament to the power of love and the human experience. With each verse, Mark invites the reader on a journey through the many facets of romantic love, from the joys and triumphs to the sorrows and struggles.

Mark's poetry is deeply personal, yet universal in its appeal. His words are carefully crafted and evocative, painting vivid imagery and evoking powerful emotions. His poems are full of longing and desire, but also of hope and resilience.

Through his work, Mark explores the complexities of love and relationships, delving into themes such as heartbreak, sacrifice, and self-discovery. His poetry is not only a reflection of his own experiences, but also a mirror for the reader, making it easy to relate to the emotions he expresses.

I highly recommend this book of Mark Bentley's romantic poetry for anyone who appreciates the beauty and power of verse. His words will stay with you long after you have finished reading, and will remind you of the importance of love in our lives.

In these poems, Mark explores the many facets of love, from the initial spark of attraction to the deep and abiding connections that can sustain us through life's trials. He writes with a rare vulnerability and honesty, baring his own emotions and experiences to the reader in a way that is both relatable and deeply moving.

But it's not just love that Mark writes about. His poems also reflect on the beauty of the natural world, and the pain of loss and grief. Through his words, he invites readers to join him on a journey of self-discovery, encouraging them to look within themselves to find their own truths.

I cannot recommend this collection of Mark Bentley's poetry enough. His words will resonate with anyone who has ever loved, lost, or simply been alive. They are a reminder that, even in the darkest of times, there is always hope, beauty, and the possibility for connection.

Dr (Col) CP Ramchandani, Ph.D

Former Director, SRM University, Chennai

15th Jan 2023

Preface

The topic of this collection of poems has been inspired by the name given by me and my first 'true love' to the narrow pathway along a lake, where we walked hand in hand for hours!

As the author of this book, I am honored to have the opportunity to share my thoughts with a wider audience. Writing poetry has been a passion of mine for many years, and this collection is a culmination of that passion.

In these pages, I explore the many facets of love, from the initial spark of attraction to the deep and abiding connections that can sustain us through life's trials. I wrote from my own experiences, but also tried to touch universal themes that we all go through. I wrote with vulnerability and honesty, baring my own emotions and experiences to the reader in a way that I hope is relatable.

As a poet, I believe in the power of words to evoke emotion and provoke thought. I believe in the ability of poetry to connect us to our deepest selves and to one another. And I believe that love is one of the most powerful and universal themes in literature.

Writing this book has been a cathartic experience for me, and I hope that readers will find something of themselves in these pages. I hope that my poetry will provide a sense of connection and understanding for those who read it. And I hope that it will inspire others to explore the depths of their own emotions and to find their own unique voice as a writer or poet.

Thank you for taking the time to read my work and for supporting me on this journey. I hope that my poetry will resonate with you and that it will be a source of inspiration for your own journey.

Mark Bentley

15th Jan 2023

Acknowledgements

I would like to express my deepest gratitude to that someone very special to me. She infuses me with never-ending love, and is my true motivation in the creation of this book of romantic poetry.

I'd also like to thank my readers, who, I'm sure, are looking for true love. Hopefully, they will find it in their lives and in these pages.

Thank you all from the bottom of my heart.

Prologue

In the pages that follow, you will find the musings of a heart in love. These poems are a reflection of the many emotions that come with the joys and sorrows of romance.

From the first flutter of attraction to the depths of heartbreak, these verses aim to capture the essence of love in all its forms.

Whether you are reading these words alone or with your beloved, may they remind you of the beauty and wonder of being human.

For in love, we are truly alive.

Enjoy!

1. An Ode to Your beauty

Your beauty shines like the sun,

With a radiance that can't be outdone.

And your smile, like a ray of light,

It warms my heart and makes everything right.

Your eyes sparkle like the stars above,

And your laughter is like a symphony of love.

Your hair flows like a gentle breeze,

And your presence is a source of peace.

You walk with grace, like a goddess divine,

And your smile, a beacon that always shines.

Your beauty, it takes my breath away,

And your smile, it brightens even the darkest day.

Oh, how blessed I am to behold,

To me your beauty is worth more than gold.

We may be far or near together,

I'll sing your praises forever.

2. The Essence of Our Love

The essence of our love is like a rose,
Ever blooming, forever glowing.
As our hearts beat in tandem,
The warmth of our embrace, with grace flowing.
The way you laugh and share my dreams,
The way you hold me tight,
I can weather any of my life's storms,
You make everything feel just right.
We're each other's safe haven,
As we lift each other up,
It's the way we make our lives better,
And fill each other's cups.
The essence of our love is pure and true,
Like a beacon in the dark.
It's the thing we can count on,
And the thing that always leaves its mark.

3. Lover's Lane

The path we walked on, hand in hand,

Our hearts and souls intertwined.

Is where my best memories remain.

We called it Lover's Lane.

In a gentle breeze, the trees remember.

As they whisper our names.

While the birds sing songs of love.

Our love had just begun.

Though we may not walk that path again,

In Lover's Lane, our love will live on.

Forever etched in the hearts of all who pass,

This testament to love will last forever.

Chapter4

I dreamt a dream with you,

In lush green fields and sky so blue,

The sun was shining bright,

With no worries in the sight.

We laughed and danced in symphony,

With hearts beating in perfect harmony,

We lay at night beneath the stars,

With our love written across the sky.

But when I woke, the dream was gone,

And I was left to face the dawn,

Still I hold that dream so dear,

For it was you, my love, I felt so near.

And although now we're far apart,

I keep that dream within my heart,

And wait for the day when we'll be free,

To dream that dream in real with thee.

Chapter5

I will never forget you,

My love for you will always be true.

In my heart, you'll forever stay,

A love like ours will never fade away.

Your smile, your laugh, your tender touch,

Memories of you, I treasure so much.

I'll hold onto every moment we shared,

For they're the ones that have truly cared.

Though life may take us down different roads,

My love for you will always hold.

I'll keep you close in every thought,

For you are the one I've dearly sought.

I will never forget you,

My love for you will always be true.

Forever and always,

my heart belongs to you.

6. Once Again, You Come To Mind

Once again you come to mind,

A memory from a different time.

A love that once was pure and true,

But now is just a memory I pursue.

Though you are gone, you still remain,

A part of me in my mind's frame.

Though I try to move on, to find my way,

My love, you come to mind and stay.

I remember the way you smiled,

You laughter, filled me with esctacy.

And when you looked into my eyes,

I was captivated in bliss forever.

But now you're gone, and I'm alone,

With nothing but your memory to hold on.

I'll keep you close, deep in my heart,

And though you're away, we'll never be apart.

Once again you come to mind,

A love that I cannot leave behind.

A memory that will always stay,

And guide me through the darkest of days.

7. How Much Do I Love You?

How much I love you, I cannot say,
For my love for you grows stronger each day.
With every breath I take, every beat of my heart,
My love for you will forever stay.
In the morning, your face is the first thing I see,
And my day is filled with Joy and esctacy.
I never knew love could be like this,
But with you, I'm truly in a life of bliss.
I love you more than words can say,
My feelings for you will never fade away.
You are in my heart, where you truly belong,
Our love is so strong, it will forever stay strong.

8. The RhyThe Rhythm of Lovethm of Love

The rhythm of our love is like a dance,

Two hearts beating, it's a perfect romance.

It ebbs and flows like the tide,

Guided by the stars on a moonlite night.

It's a symphony of passion and grace,

A melody nothing can replace.

The rhythm of our hearts beating as one,

A heavenly feeling of love that's just begun.

It's the way you look at me,

The way you hold my hand.

It's the way you make me feel,

Like I'm the only person in land.

The cadency of our love is a beautiful feeling,

Like a melody we will forever sing.

It's the rhythm that makes our hearts beat,

A love and longing that is truly sweet.

9. You Make My World Come Al

Your bright and shining eyes,
Light up my darkest days.
You make my world come alive,
And chase away my fears and dismays.
Your touch is like a spark,
That ignites a flame within my heart.
Your love is like a beacon,
Guiding me through the darkest of seasons.
You make my world come alive,
With your laughter and your smile.
You fill my heart with joy,
And make my life worthwhile.

10. The Reason for My Song

You are the reason for my song,

The melody that echoes in my heart.

With every beat, my love grows strong,

Wish you had never gone apart.

About you, very word that I write,

Ignites a spark of insight.

Your face, your smile, your gentle embrace,

Leave me in a state of pure grace.

You inspire me to reach the sky,

With you by my side, I know I can fly,

And chase my dreams, and never stop.

Till with you together, we reach the top.

My songs are a tribute to you, my love,

You are the melody of my life.

For you are the reason my heart sings,

The songs of love, and my world looks bright.

11. The Sights That We Loved

The sights that we loved together,
Remain in my heart forever.
The sound of the waves, the smell of the sea,
The warmth of the sun, and your company.
We walked on the beach, hand in hand,
As the sun set on the golden sand.
We talked and we laughed, we shared our dreams,
In those moments, everything it seemed.
The sights that we loved together,
Always remind me of you,
The feelings we shared, the love that we found,
Is always with me all the day around.
Though we are now apart,
Those memories of you always start,
Bring a smile on my face,
And a warmth in my heart.

12. When You Smile

When you smile, it lights up my world,
Like the sun breaking through the clouds.
Your eyes sparkle, and your cheeks flush,
And all my worries disappear in a hush.
Your laughter is like music to my ears,
It fills me with joy and banishes all fears.
With you by my side, everything feels right,
Together, our future is so bright.
So keep on smiling, my dear,
For in your smile, I find my cheer.
With every grin, my worries disappear,
And I am left with your memories so clear.

13. Holding You in My Arms

In your embrace, my heart sings,
A melody of blissful love, pure and true.
With every beat, my soul sings,
Songs of eternal love anew.
The warmth of your body,
The scent of your hair.
The feel of your skin,
All these sensations, oh so rare.
The world around me disappears
As I lose myself in your thoughts.
In these moments, there are no fears
Only the beauty of our love, that I saught.
As I hold you me in your arms so tight,
We dance to the rhythm of our hearts
In your embrace,
Every moment feels just so right.

14. Listen to my heart

Listen to my heart, and hear its gentle beat

As it sings a song of love, its melody is so sweet

With each thump, a message it sends

Of the love that it holds, till the very end

Listen to my heart, hear its whispers low

Of the longing and the aching, it wants you to know

For in your absence, it feels incomplete

And in your presence, it skips a beat

Listen to my heart, hear the rhythm it makes

As it beats in time with your heart's own pace

For when we're together, our hearts are in sync

And our love story, becomes a beautiful epic

Listen to my heart, as it call out your name

It yearns to be with you, again and yet again.

For in you, it has found its home,

And in your love, it forever will roam.

So listen to my heart, hear it sing

Of the love, it holds for you, which is everything.

15. Your Beauty

Your beauty, like a rose in bloom,
Makes my heart sing with joy and glee,
It's a sight, that makes my senses swoon,
And fills my soul with ecstasy.
Your eyes, like pools of liquid gold,
Reflect the light of the stars above,
They hold a story, yet untold,
Of love and beauty, that I love.
Your smile, like a ray of sunshine,
Brightens my day and chases away the night,
Your beauty is truly divine,
Makes my day complete and every moment so fine.
Your grace, like a melody, so sweet,
Will forever play in my own heartbeat.

16. The Feel of your Lips

The feel of your lips lingers on,

Etched in my memory, forever strong.

Every kiss is a sweet reminder,

Of the love that we have always longed.

In every breath I take,

I can feel your lips on mine,

A gentle touch that never fades,

And your love that forever stays.

Your lips, have the taste of paradise,

Make my senses come alive, and my soul surmise.

With every kiss, my heart sings,

And soars on melodies love brings.

As the days go by,

I'm lost in your thoughts,

As your lips brush on mine,

My heart races and our soul entwine.

The feel of your lips,

Is etched in my heart.

And every kiss, reminds of a promise,

Never to drift apart.

17. Be Mine Forever

Be mine forever, my sweetheart,
Let our souls unite forever, never drift apart.
In your eyes, my future is so bright,
With you by my side, everything feels just right.
With every beat of my heart, I know
That you are the one I want much more.
I promise to love you all of time
To be yours forever and you'll be mine.
With every kiss, every touch, every sigh,
I feel my love for you multiply
You are my sun, my moon, my stars above
You are my guide, my world, my love.
As we walk through life's journey,
Together, facing all, with just no worry
Forever bound by our hearts, our souls, our fate
Be mine forever, my love, my mate.

18. Joys of Love

The joys of love are like a symphony
Each moment a new melody
A crescendo of happiness and delight
As our hearts take flight
With every touch and every kiss
Our love for each other is nothing less
Than pure magic, a wonder to behold
A love story, forever to be told
The joys of love are like the first spring
A season of new beginnings
A time for growth and a new life
As our love blossoms, free from strife
With every laugh and every smile
Our love for each other is worth the while
As we walk through life, side by side
The joys of love, our hearts abide.
The joys of love are like a song
Sweet and heartwarming that plays along
As we dance through life, hand in hand
Our love will forever endure and withstand.

19. My Never-ending Love

My endless love for you, like the ocean wide

It knows no bounds, it cannot hide

It flows within me, a constant tide

A love that will forever abide

Like the stars in the sky, it shines bright

Guiding me through the darkest night

Our love burns with fierce might

Its a love that will always be in sight

My endless love for you, like a rose

It blossoms and grows, forever chose

A love that's true, pure and whole

A love that will never grow old

With every breath and every beat

My love for you, cannot be beat

It's an unbreakable bond, complete

My endless love for you, so sweet

My endless love for you is like a light

Guiding me and illuminates the darkest night

It will be the reason to keep going on

And it will last forever, till the dawn.

20. A Walk in the Clouds

A walk in the clouds, with you by my side
Is like a dream, where love is the guide
With your hand in mine, your heart so true
I'm walking on clouds, because of you.
As we stroll through the clouds, arm in arm
In you I've found my love and my charm
The world below us seems so small
As we rise above it all
With every step, we leave behind
All the doubts and fears of our mind
With you by my side, I can face anything
A walk in the clouds, with you, is like heavens singing.
Our love is a journey, a walk in the clouds
Where we can find peace and our hearts are proud
Forever together, forever we'll soar
On the wings of love, forever more.

21. Never-ending Love

A love that's forever, a love that's true
A never-ending love, is what I found in you
With every kiss, every touch, every beat
I feel my love for you, grow and repeat
Like the waves on the shore, it never ends
A love that transcends, all time and bends
With every sunrise, and every sunset
My devotion to you, I will never forget.
A never-ending love, like a river that flows
It ebbs and it flows, it never slows
With every moment, every day
My love for you, in every single way
Like the stars in the sky, it shines bright
A love that will last, through the darkest night
With every breath, every heartbeat
I know my love for you, will never retreat.
A never-ending love, that's what I found in you
A love that's pure and true, at life's every bend.
I'll love you today, tomorrow, and always,
My love for you is eternal, and will never end.

22. The Gift of Your Love

The gift of your love is a treasure to me
A precious gem it will always be.
With every kiss, every touch, every moment
My love for you, it never will be broken.
With your love, I can sore and fly
Touch the sky and reach for the stars high
With your love, I will achieve everything
And ballads of love I will sing.
The gift of your love, is a treasure indeed
Our love that will always be.
With your love, I feel so alive,
I know that our love will thrive.
The gift of your love, is like a breath of fresh air
A light in the darkness, a love that's always fair
It's a treasure that I'll always hold dear
A love that will last all time and always be here.

23. Don't Ever Go

Don't ever go, my love, my heart
For without you, my world will fall apart
With you by my side, I feel complete
And I know our love will forever be sweet
Don't ever go, my one and only
For you are my life, and destiny
Without you, my life would be lonely
With you, our love will only grow.
Don't ever go, my love, my light
For you guide me through the darkest night
Our love will last, through all time
Forever yours and forever mine.

24. Your Perfume Lingers On

Your perfume lingers on, a sweet reminder
Of the love we shared, the memories we kinder
In every breath, I smell your scent
And my heart aches with a love so intense
Your perfume lingers on, like a ghost
A haunting presence, I love the most
With every step, I feel you near
And my heart yearns for you to be here
Your perfume lingers on, a symbol of our past
A love that will forever last
With every sniff, I remember your touch
And I long for you, so much
With every breath, I feel you near
And I'll always hold you dear
Your perfume lingers on, a reminder of you
A love that will always be true.

25. A Glimpse of Your Smile

A glimpse of your smile, is like a ray of sunshine
It brightens my day and makes everything fine
With just a curve of your lips, my heart skips a beat
And I feel the warmth, so sweet.
A glimpse of your smile, is a sight to behold
It's a window to your soul, as pure as gold
With every flash of your grin, my worries fade away
And I feel a sense of joy, here to stay.
A glimpse of your smile, is like a breath of fresh air
It fills me with hope, and I know you're here
With every beam of your smile, I feel alive
And I know that everything will be alright.
A glimpse of your smile, is a treasure to me
It's a reminder of our love and our destiny
With every smile, I feel your love
And it's enough to make my heart soar above.

26. The Maze of Life

The maze of life can be winding and confusing
With twists and turns, and often illusions
But with you by my side, I know I'll find my way
For your love is a beacon, that guides my way.
With our love as the guide, we'll navigate life's winding path
With our love as the map, we'll overcome any aftermath
We'll face the challenges, and overcome the fears
For our love is a force, that nothing can bear
The maze of life, can be dark and lonely
But with you by my side, I'm never alone.
With every step, I feel your touch
And I know that I'm loved, very so much.
The maze of life is a journey worth taking
With you by my side, my heart is yours for the taking
Forever and always, my love, my sweetheart
In this maze of life, we'll never part.

27. Your Lustrous Locks and Beautiful Smile

Your lustrous locks and beautiful smile,

Takes my breath away,

Your beauty is beyond compare,

A treasure that I'll always hold dear.

Your hair, flows like a river of sunlight,

Is truly a sight to behold,

And your smile is like sunshine,

A true reflection of your soul.

With every movement with the breeze,

Your locks sway and shine,

A smile perfect, so truly rare,

Your beauty is truly divine,

28. Holding You Close

Holding you close, in the splendor of the moon,
Is like a dream, that's come true soon
With the moonlight shining down on us
Our love feels like it's been sanctified, thus.
The soft glow of the moon, upon your face
Is a sight that I'll always embrace
Your head on my chest, and my arms around you
I feel like the luckiest person, that I knew
The splendor of the moon, it's a beautiful thing
But holding you close, is what makes my heart sing
With every beat, I feel your love
And I know our love is sent from above.

29. As Our Love Mingles

As your love mingles with mine,

Like a symphony, that is divine,

Each note, a feeling of pure bliss,

Each chord, a promise of eternal kiss.

Our love, a perfect blend,

A harmony, that never ends,

As our hearts beat as one,

Our love, forever begun.

Our souls, entwined,

In a love that is unrefined,

A love that is pure and true,

A love that will forever be new.

As our love mingles, it grows stronger,

A bond that will last even longer,

Through the highs and the lows,

Our love will forever glow.

As your love mingles with mine,

I know that I'll be forever thine,

For a love like ours, is rare,

And I'll cherish it, forever, with care.

30. Mysterious Vibes

The mysterious vibes of our love,
Is a feeling hard to describe,
Such a pull towards each other,
Is only felt deep inside.
Our love is like a magnet,
Drawing us closer every day,
A force that's beyond explanation,
In a unique and special way.
The mysterious vibes of our love,
Are like a symphony, that's played,
A harmony that's in perfect sync,
A love that's truly made.
It's a feeling, hard to put into words,
But it's there, in every touch,
Unexplainable and mysterious, yet
It is so real, and cherished so much.

31. The Light of Your Love

The light of your love, illuminates my soul
It guides me through the darkness,
and makes me whole.
With every breath, and the beat of my heart
I feel your love, which is so sweet.
The light of your love is like sunshine,
That touches my heart,
and makes my world divine.
The light of your love is a guiding force
Your love is a treasure
That I truly care.